FLOWERS TO COLOUR

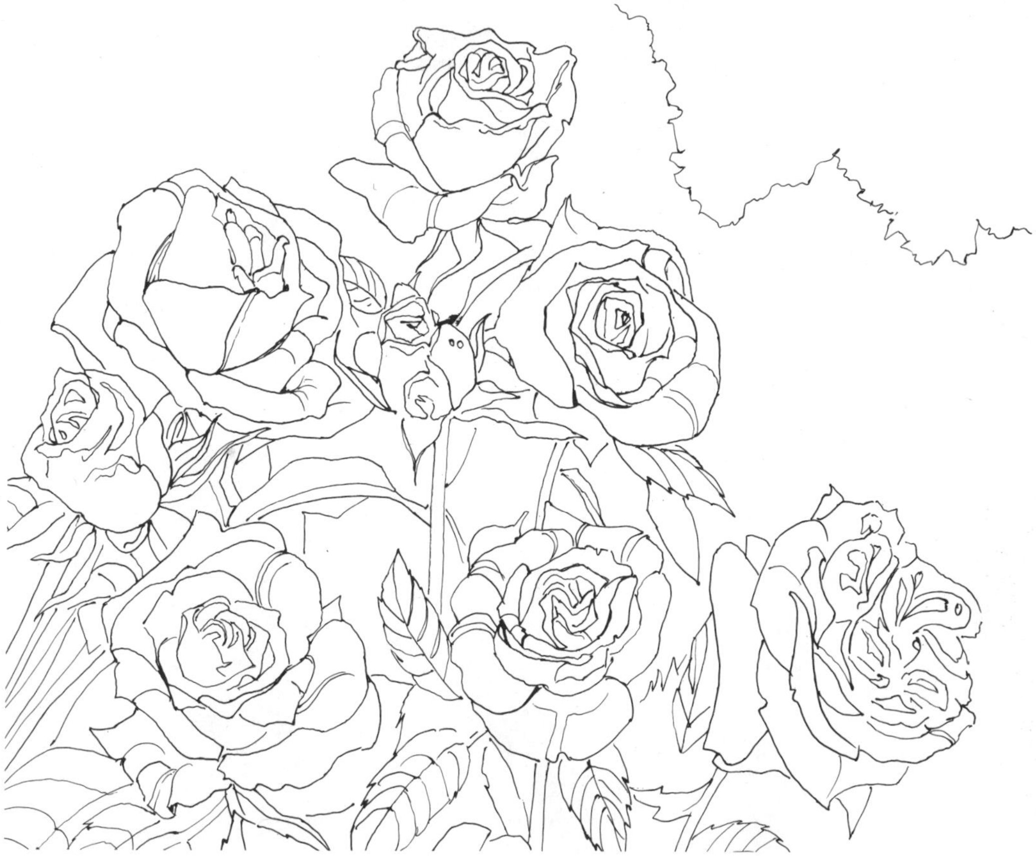

Published by: W. F. GRAHAM (NORTHAMPTON) LTD.
Illustrated by: JACKIE NEWTON, THURSO, SCOTLAND
Printed by: PHÖNIX DRUCK GMBH LEIPZIG, GERMANY

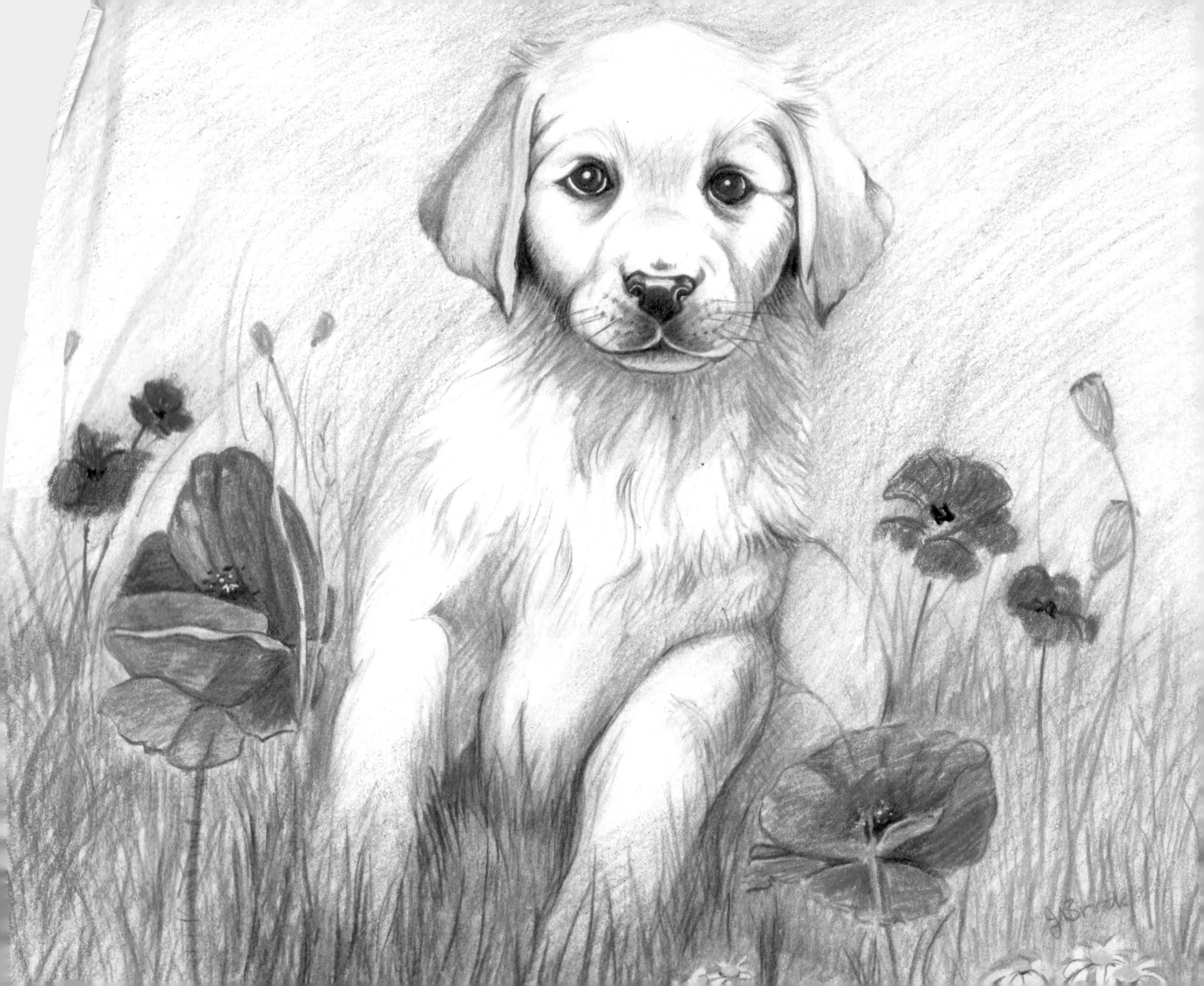

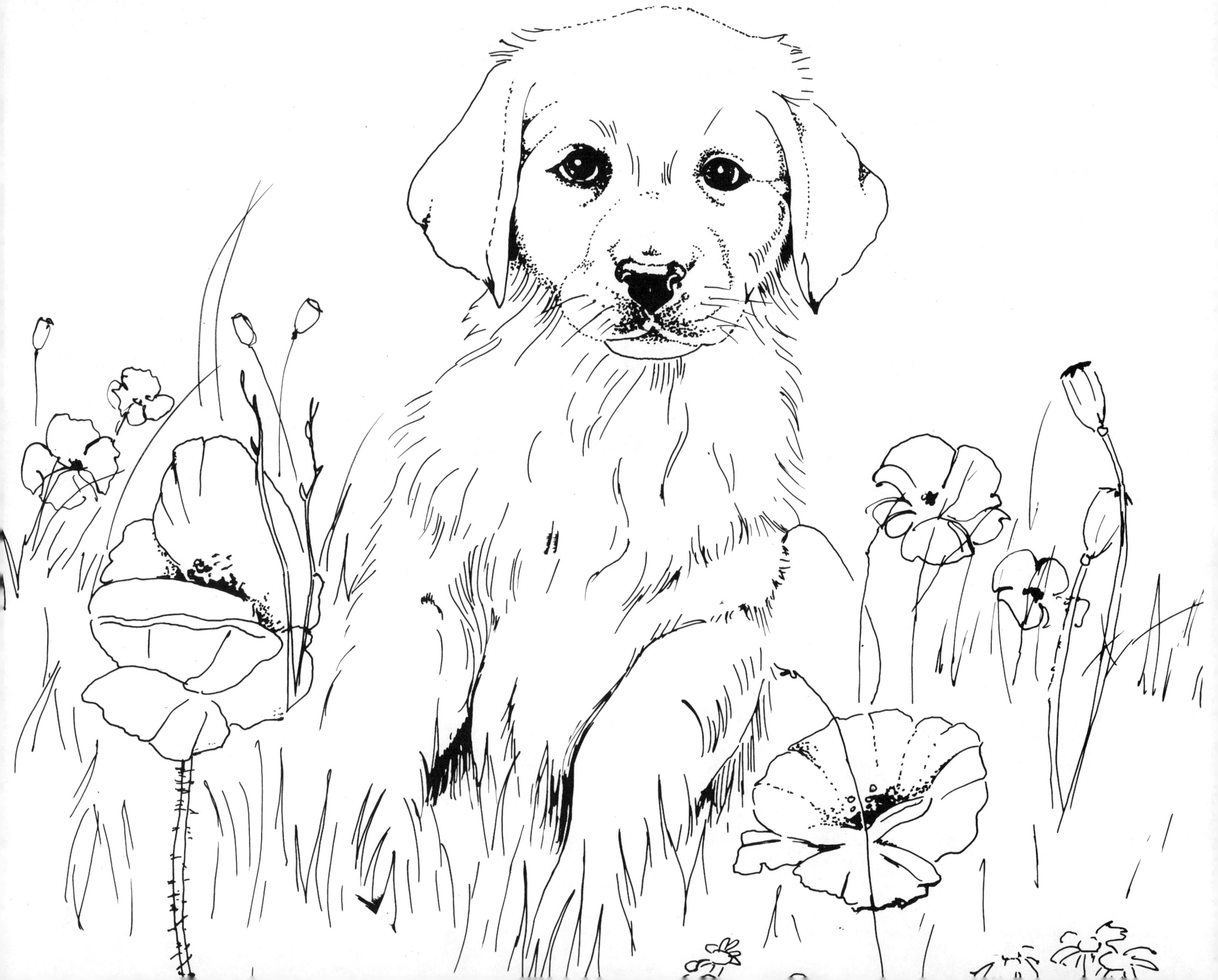

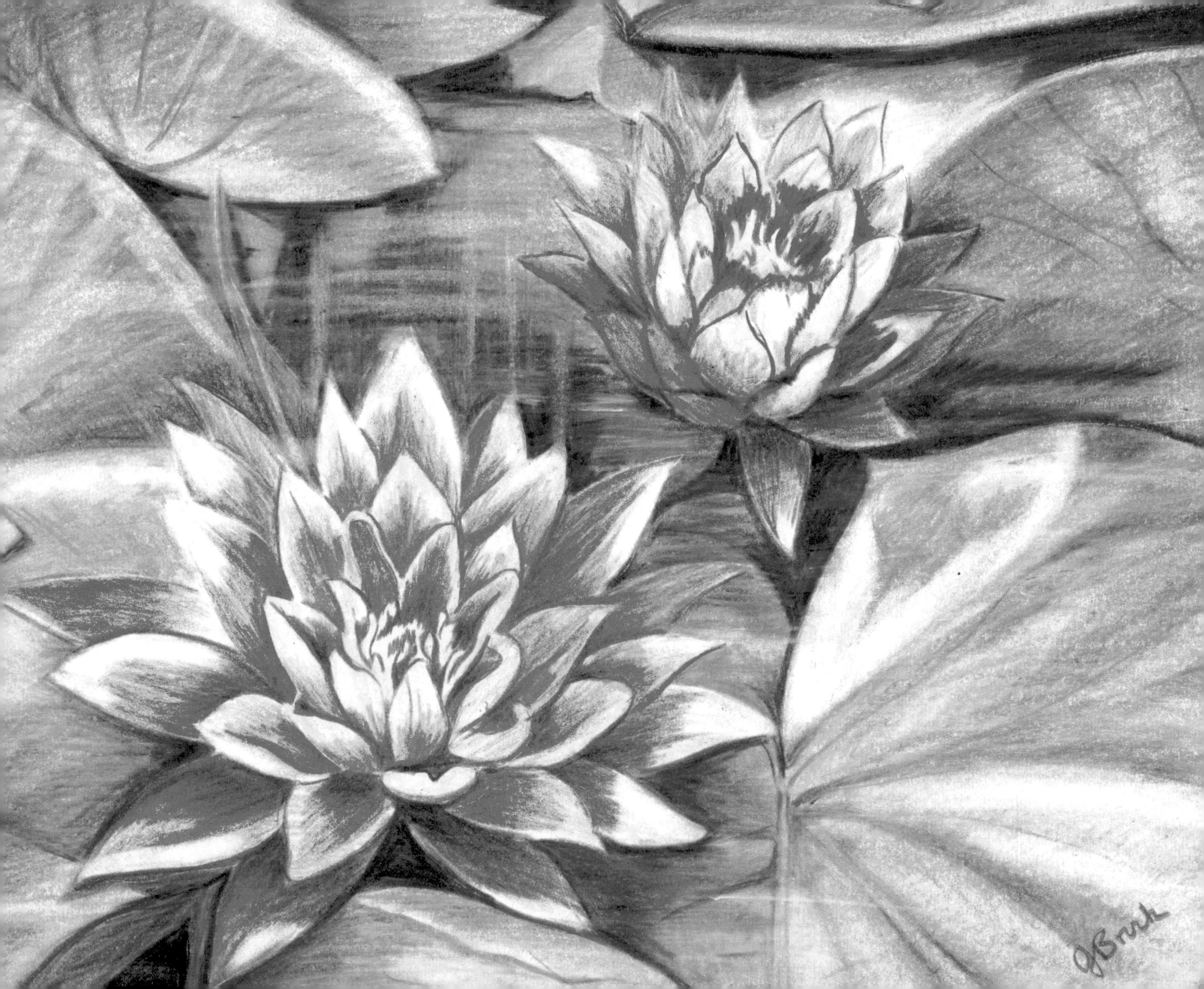

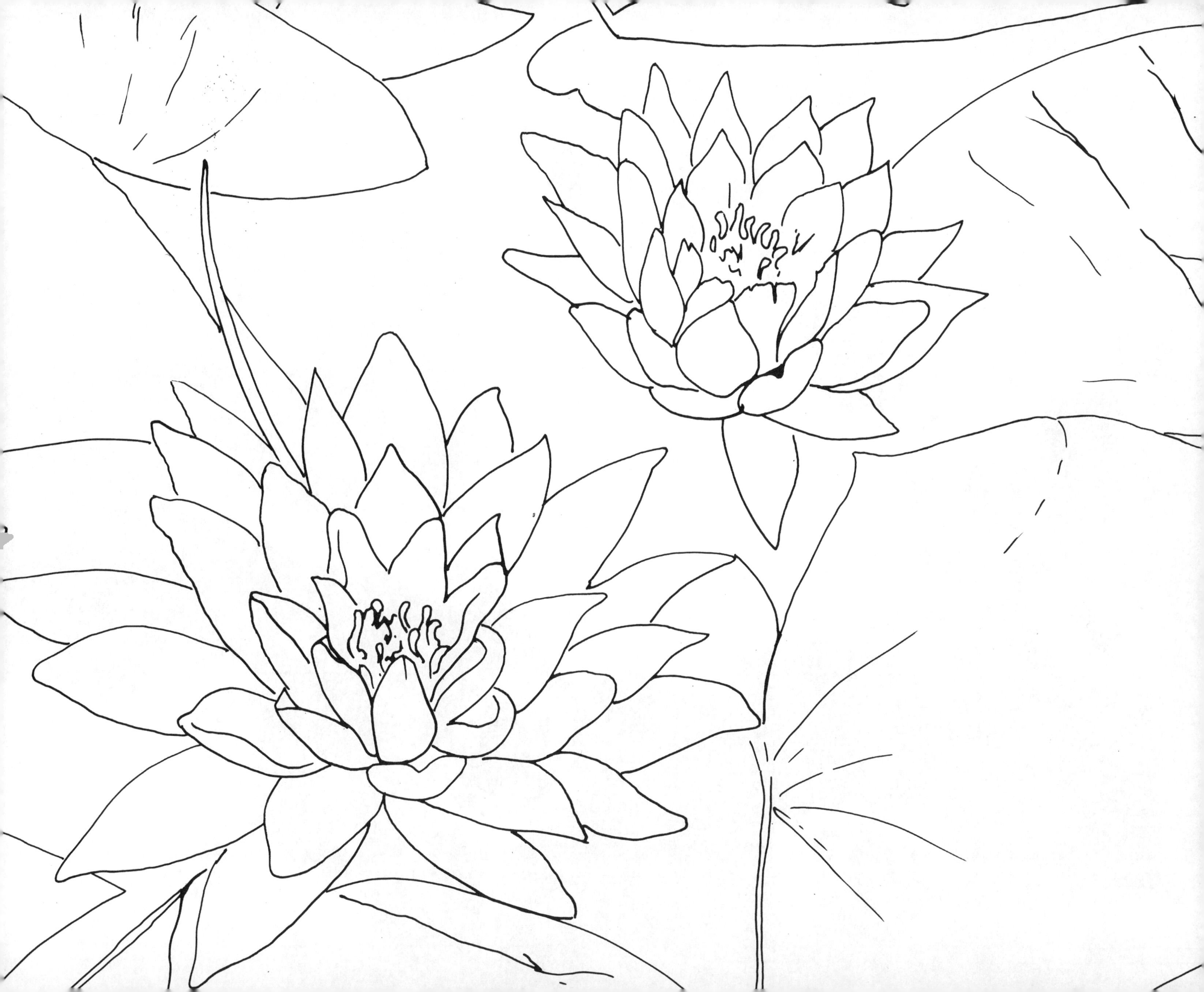

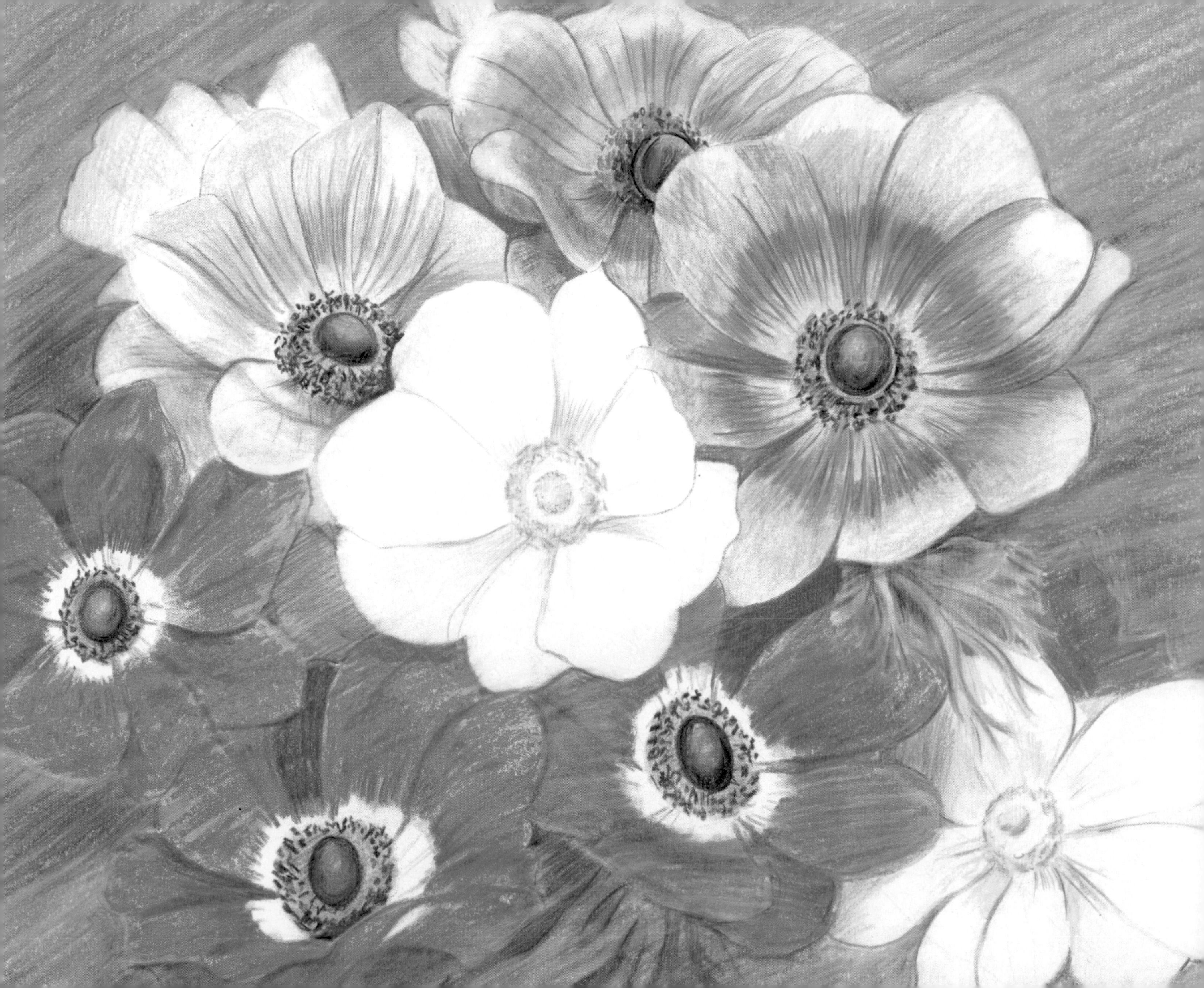

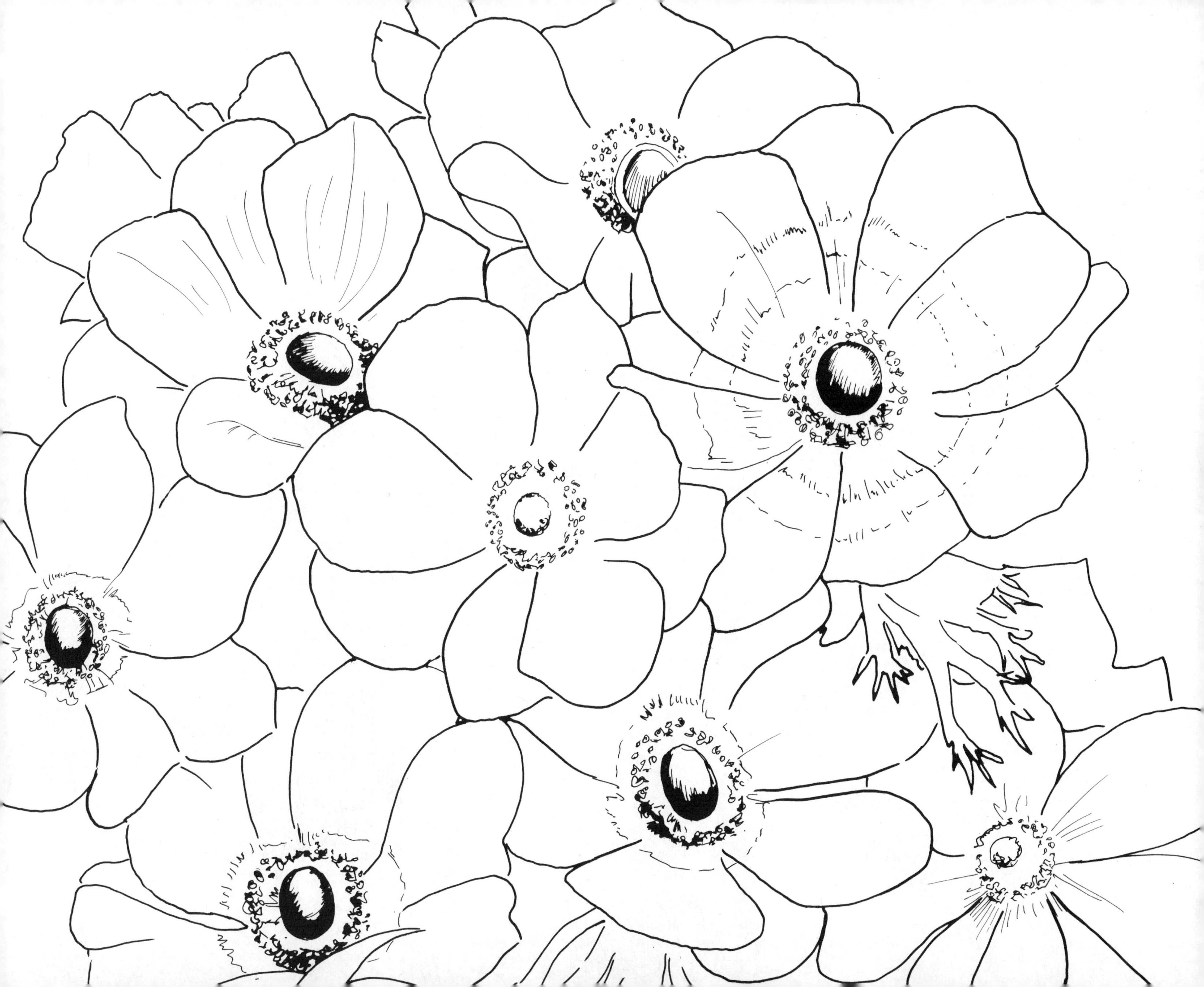

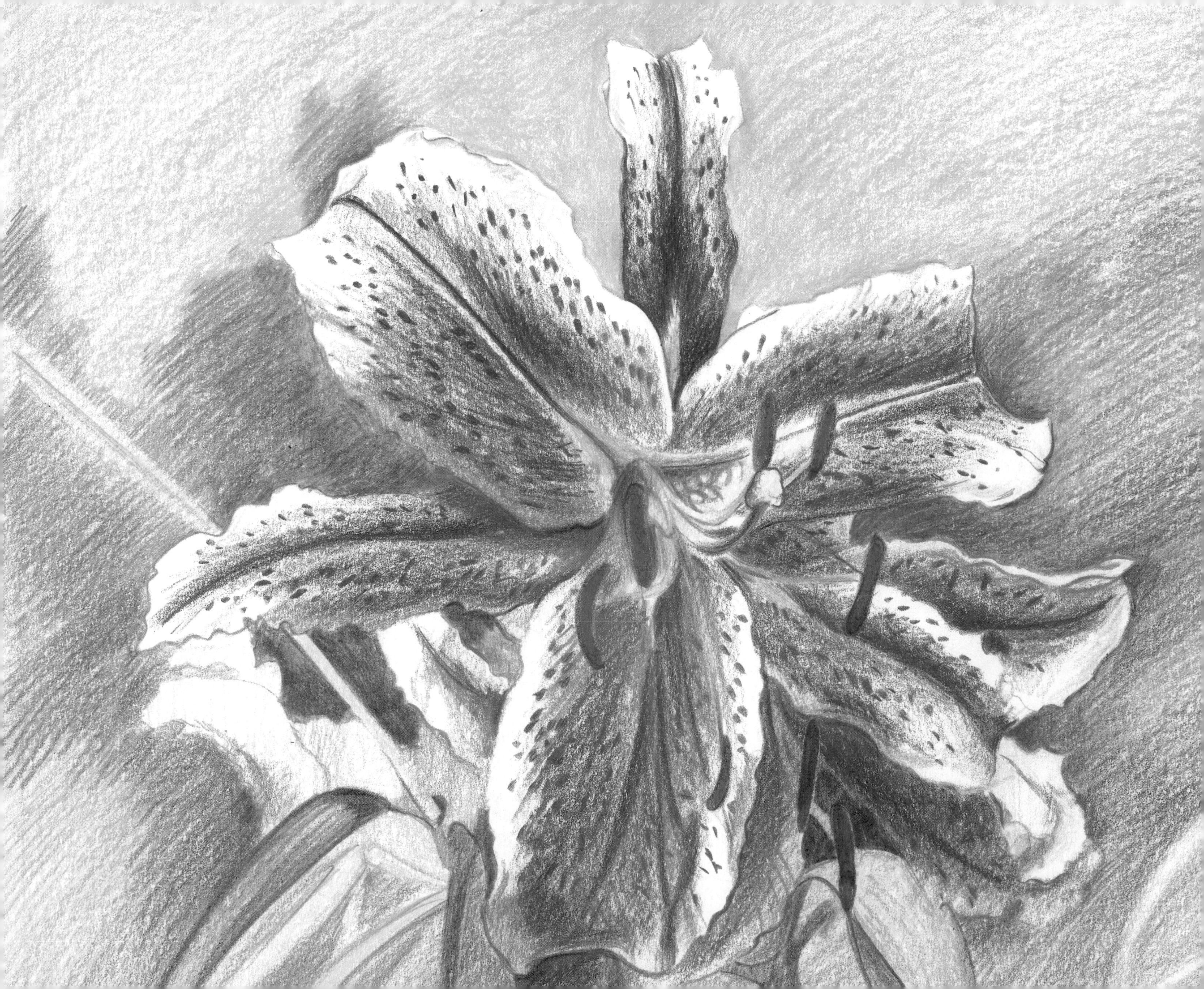

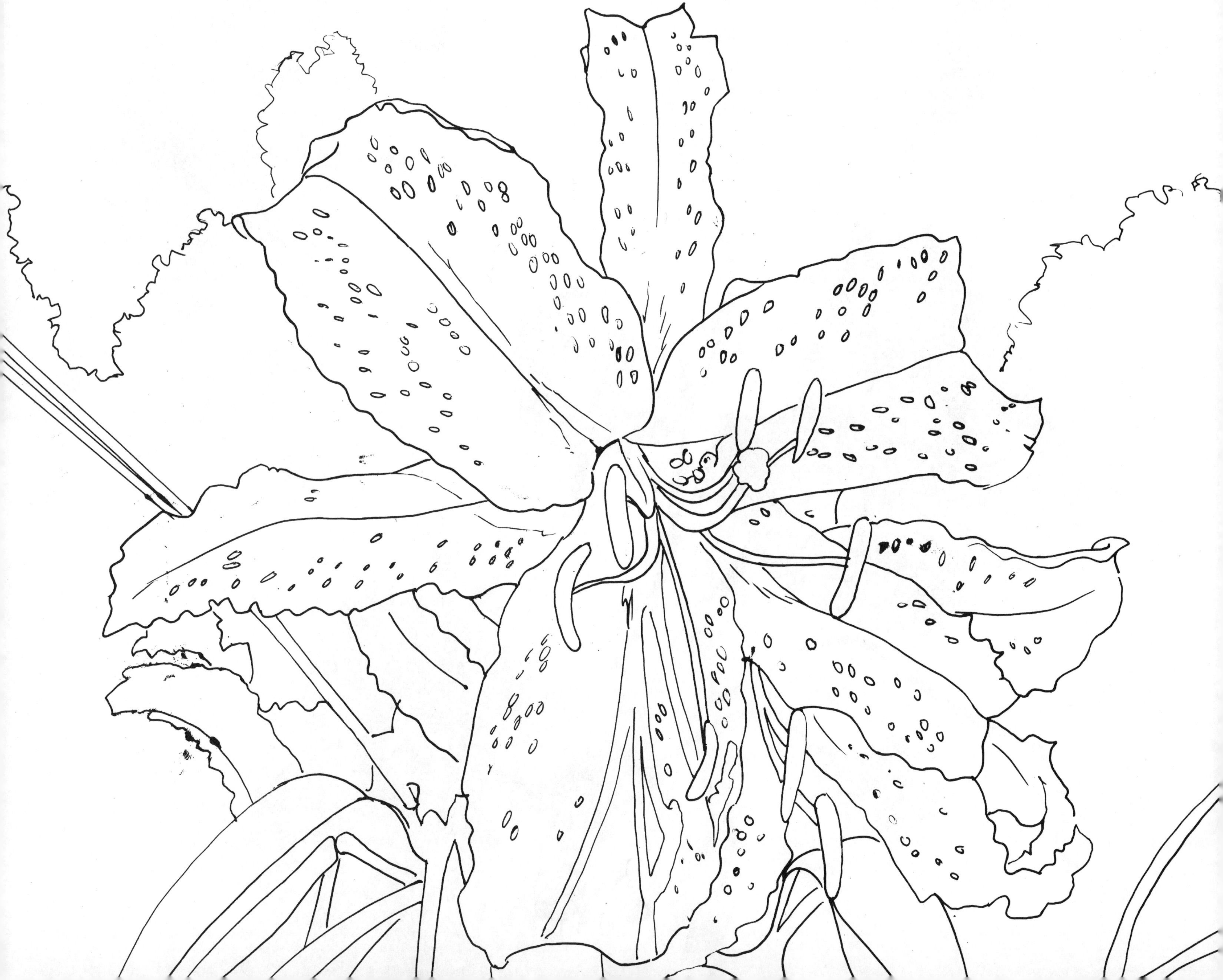

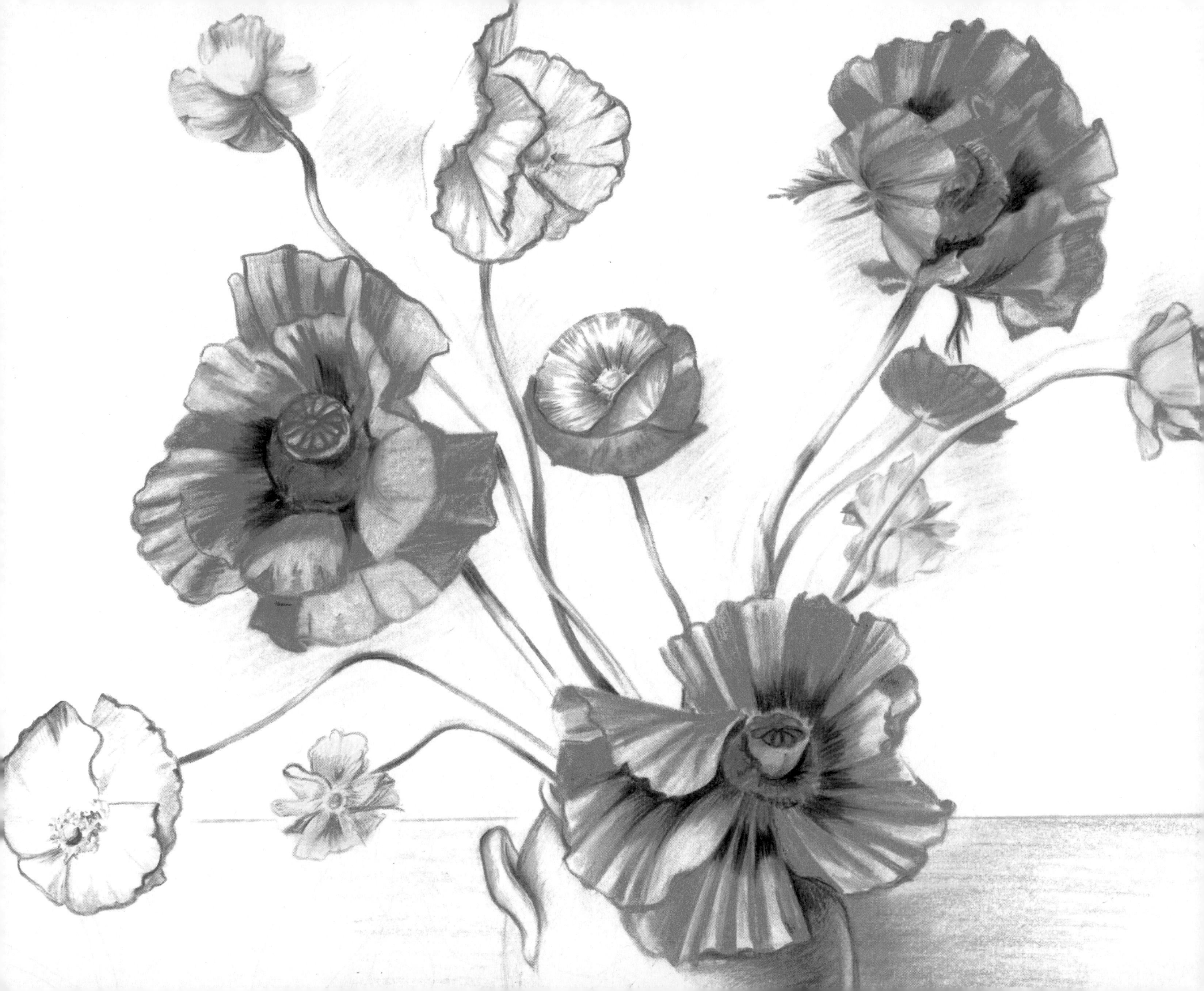

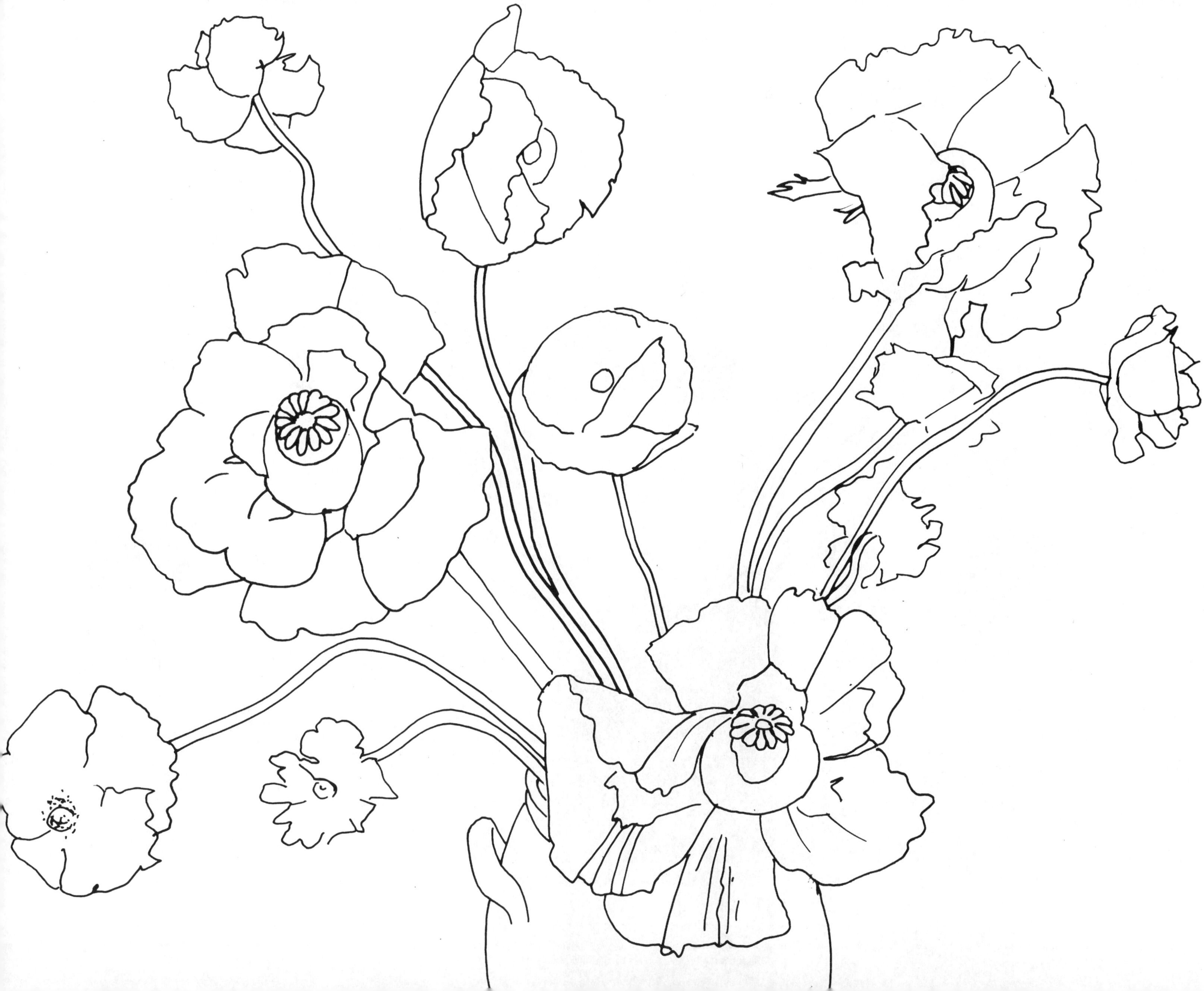

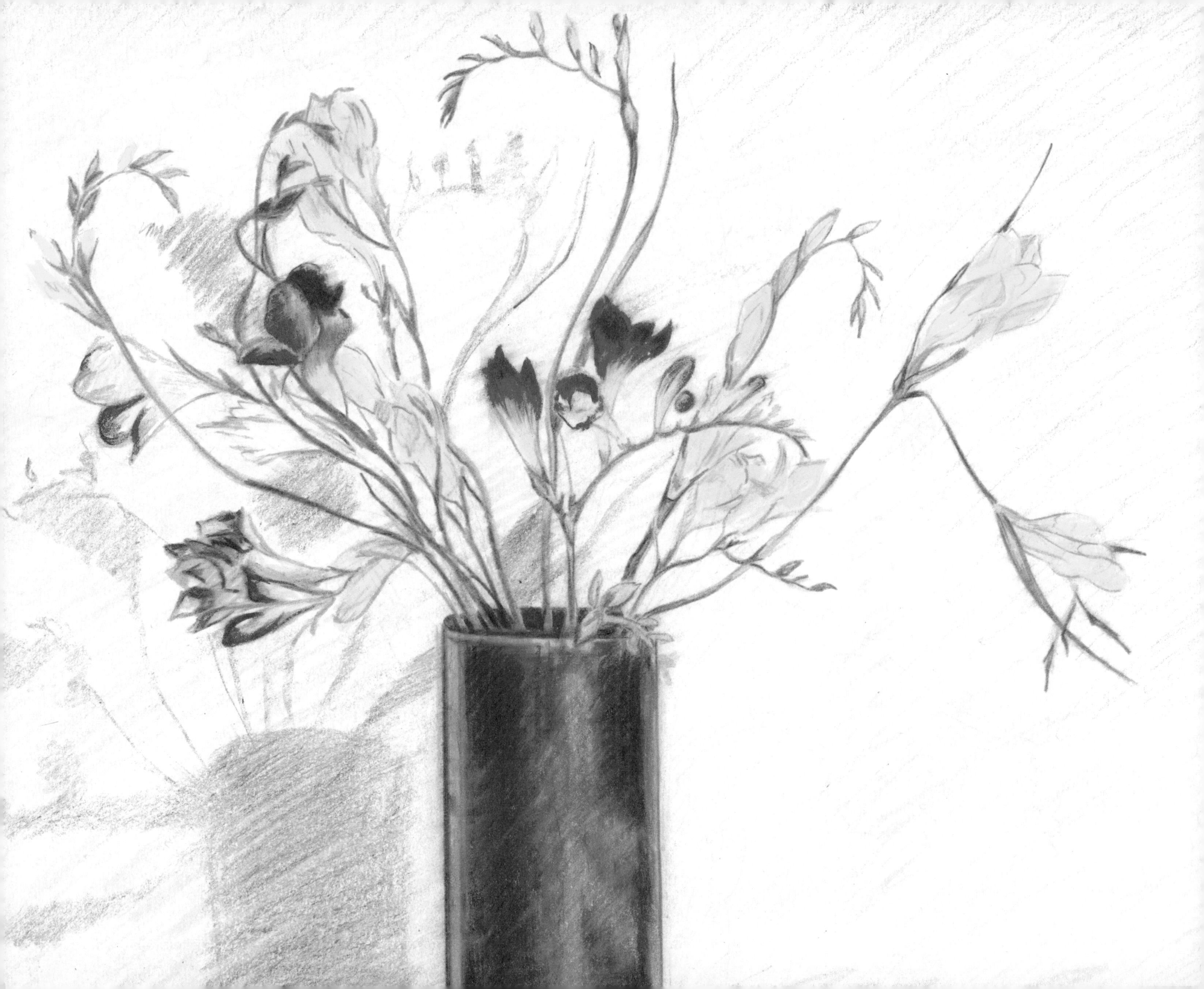

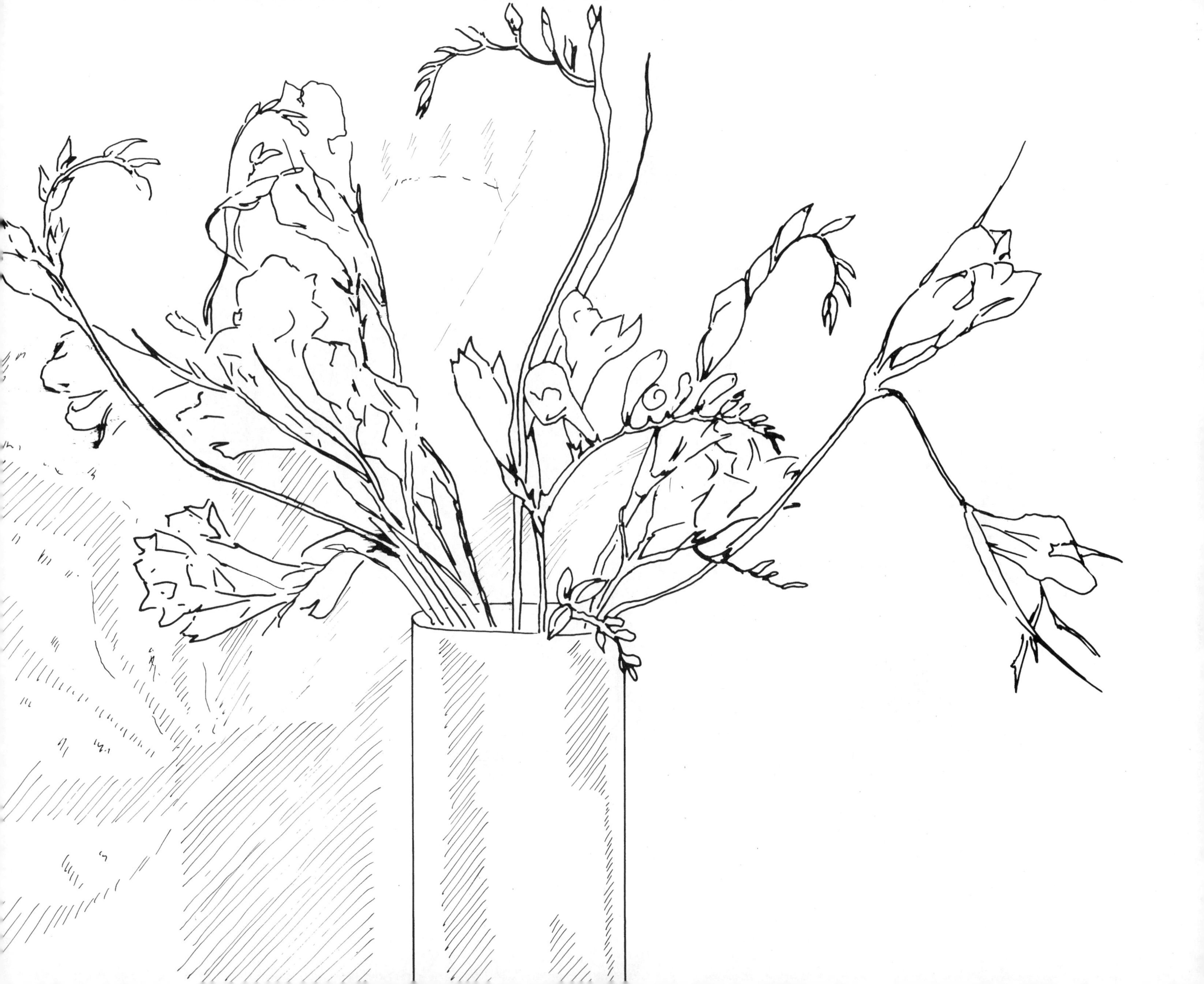

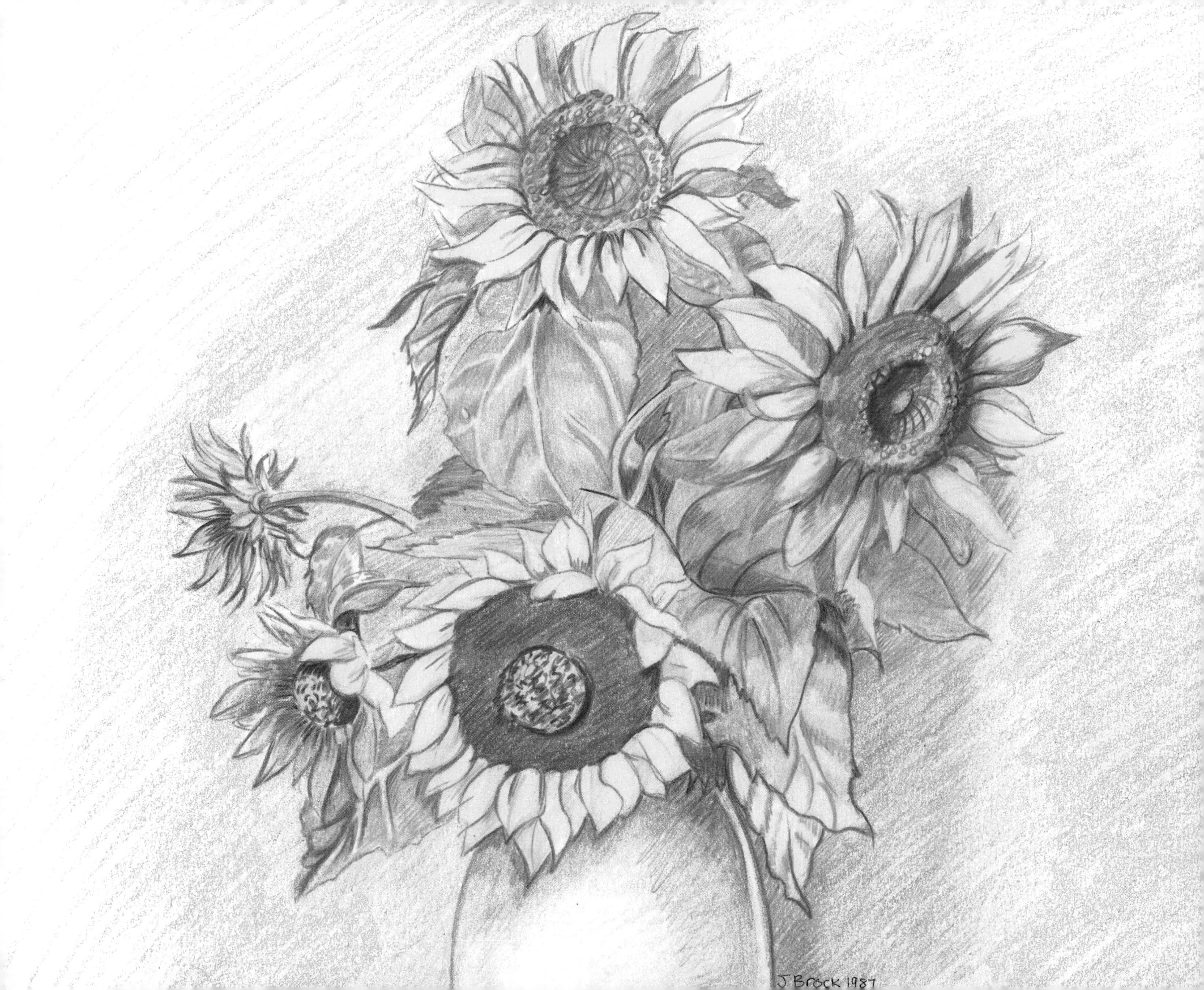
J.Brock 1987

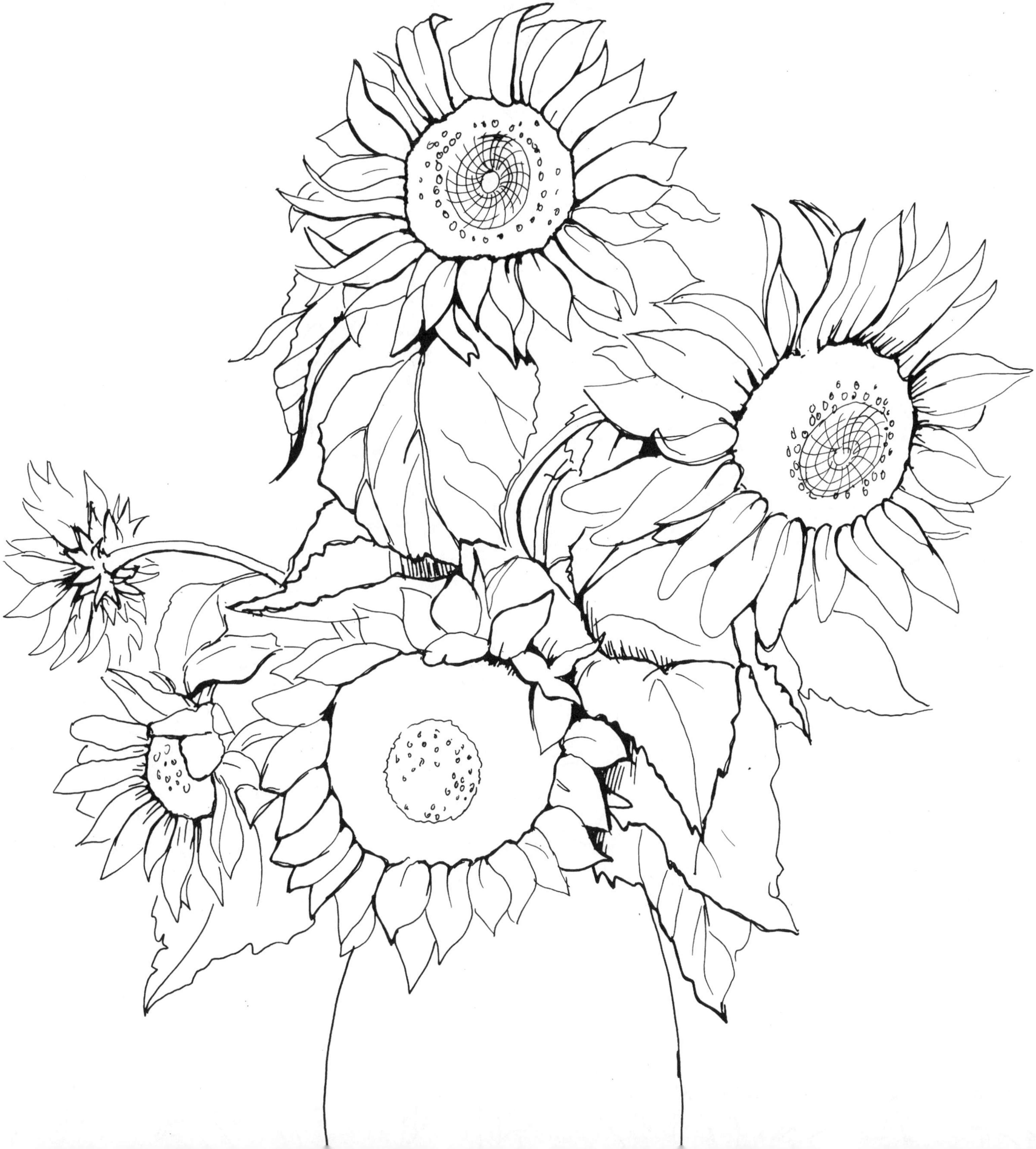

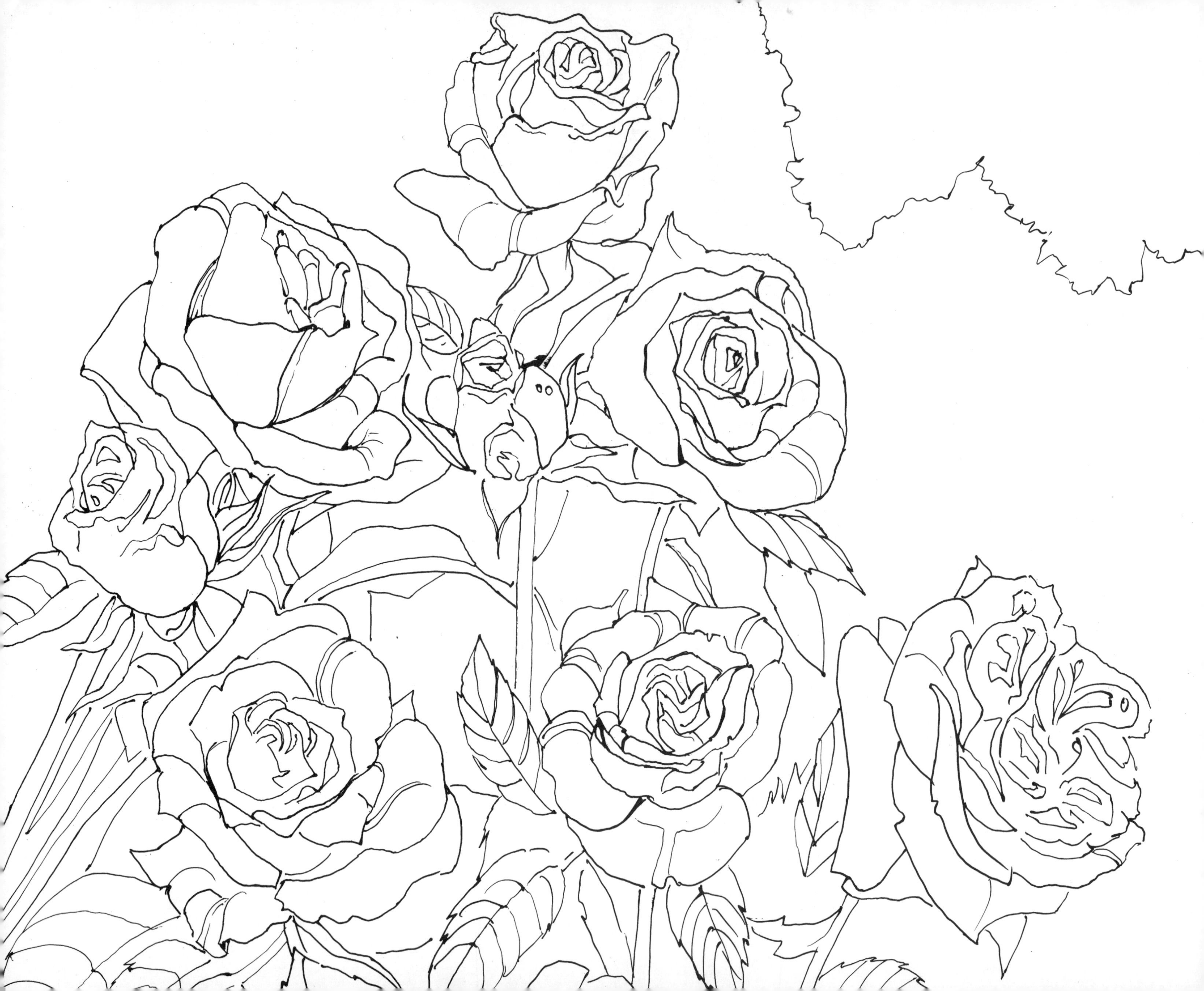